apples &
chalkdust
notes

Vicki Caruana, *America's Teacher*

An *Apples & Chalkdust™* Book

08 07 06 05 04 03   10 9 8 7 6 5 4 3 2 1

Apples & Chalkdust Notes—
Fun and Encouraging Notes from Teachers to Students
ISBN 1-56292-381-1

Copyright © 2003 Vicki Caruana

Published by Honor Books
An Imprint of Cook Communications Ministries
4050 Lee Vance View
Colorado Springs, CO 80918

Developed by Bordon Books
6532 E. 71st Street, Suite 105
Tulsa, OK 74133

Dear Teacher,

I'm so happy that you have this gem in your hands. A teacher's day is full of words, but sometimes it's nice if someone else provides them.

School-related notes tend to be all about excuses. Everyone appreciates love notes. Use these as love notes to your students. *Apples & Chalkdust Notes* is a creative tool to inspire and encourage your students—the reason you do what you do.

Look around your classroom and you'll find a perfect match for a special note. Don't make a big deal when you give it to them. Private praise can be so much more powerful than public praise.

I hope that your note giving is the start of a very practical and promising practice.

May God Bless You in Abundance,

Vicki Caruana

Follow the steps below to turn these pages into special notes from you to your students.

1 Remove a note from the book.

Personalize it in any way you wish. **2**

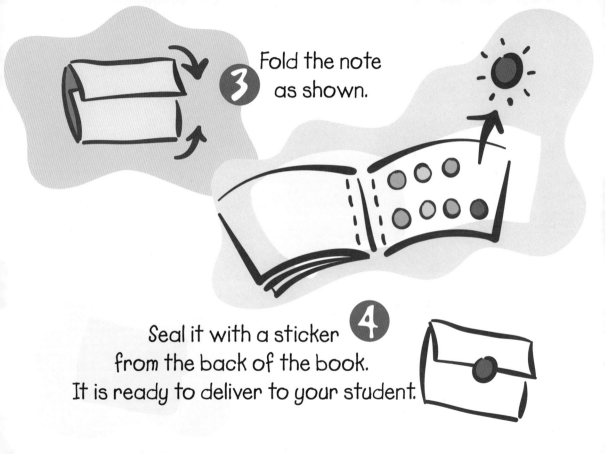

Fold the note as shown.

Seal it with a sticker from the back of the book. It is ready to deliver to your student.

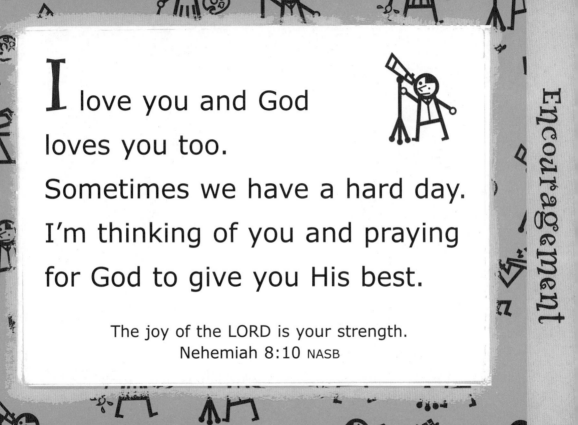

I love you and God loves you too.
Sometimes we have a hard day.
I'm thinking of you and praying
for God to give you His best.

The joy of the LORD is your strength.
Nehemiah 8:10 NASB

Encouragement

For:

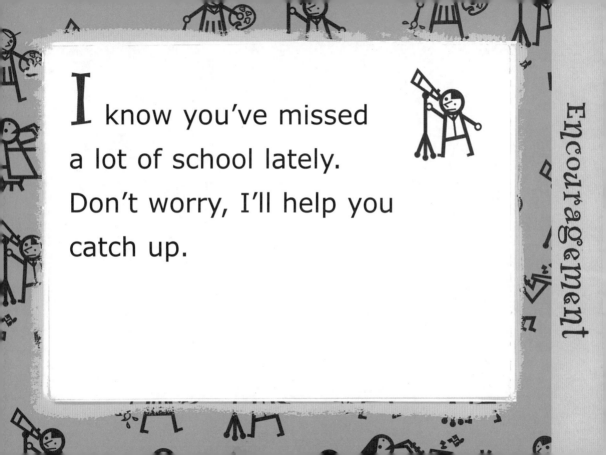

I know you've missed a lot of school lately. Don't worry, I'll help you catch up.

For:

I remember what it is like to be the new kid in school. It won't be long before you know everyone!

For:

I know there aren't many other boys in our class this year. That just makes you more special!

For:

I know there aren't many other girls in our class this year. That just makes you more special!

For:

You've seemed a little sad lately. I will pray for you for as long as you need me to.

Pray for each other.
James 5:16 NIV

For:

I know it's hard to move away, but you make friends so easily. I know you'll make some great friends quickly in your new school!

For:

Friendships are stronger than you think. Give it some time and things will work out just fine.

A friend loves at all times.
Proverbs 17:17 NASB

For:

I know you didn't do as well on your test as you had hoped. Let's work together so you can do better next time.

For:

You are different. You are special. Without you this would be a very boring class!

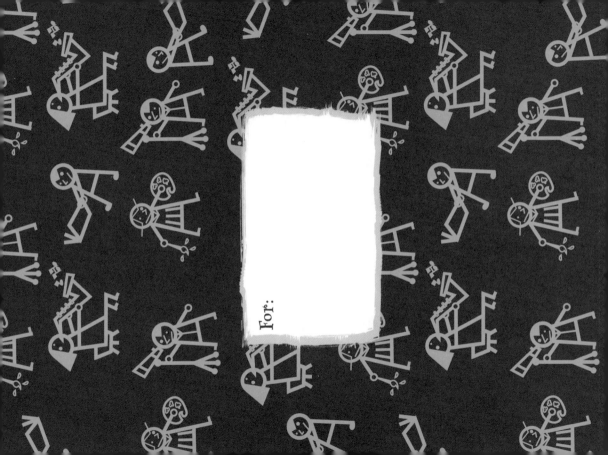

For:

I missed your happy heart in class. I'm so glad you're back with us.

For:

You are my sunshine!
I missed your smiling
face today.

For:

I didn't laugh much today because you weren't here. I missed you!

For:

You only missed a test, but we all missed you!

I Missed You

For:

I know you were sick and had to stay home. We were lost without you!

For:

Even the fish in the fish tank missed you! That says a lot.

For:

The field trip just wasn't the same without you. We missed having you along.

For:

I missed your quick answers today! I missed your raised hand, ready to share something special with us all.

For:

I wasn't the only one who missed you today. Your best friend looked so lonely.

A+

For:

It was too quiet today without you. Your laughter warms my heart. You were missed.

For:

Knock Knock
Who's there?
Aardvark!
Aardvark who?
Aardvark a hundred miles for one of your smiles!

For:

This coupon entitles the bearer to one day of no homework on any day they choose! That means you!

For:

Great news! Teacher says we have a test today come rain or shine. So what's so great about that? It's snowing outside!

For:

Teacher: And what did you learn during the summer?

Pupil: I learned that three months is not enough time to straighten up my room.

For:

Check the appropriate homework excuse:

○ I put it in a safe and lost the combination.

○ I loaned it to a friend who suddenly moved away.

○ My little sister ate it.

For:

This coupon entitles the bearer to 10 extra minutes of recess with a friend!

For:

This coupon entitles the bearer to one day of no homework on any day they choose! That means you!

For:

A pencil without an eraser may as well be just a pen.

For:

This coupon entitles the bearer to eat lunch with the teacher today! And we're having take-out pizza!

For:

This coupon entitles the bearer to eat lunch with the teacher today! And we're having take-out pizza!

For:

Out of all the people in the world, there is no one like you. God made you special, and I am so glad He put you in my class.

For:

The art teacher showed me your work. It is quite impressive!

For:

You always seem to be able to make peace with others. You make our classroom a wonderful place to be.

For:

You have a way with words. Your stories are always so interesting to read!

For:

You are one of the best math students I have ever had. Your mind works so quickly!

For:

You have a beautiful singing voice. Use it often to make others smile.

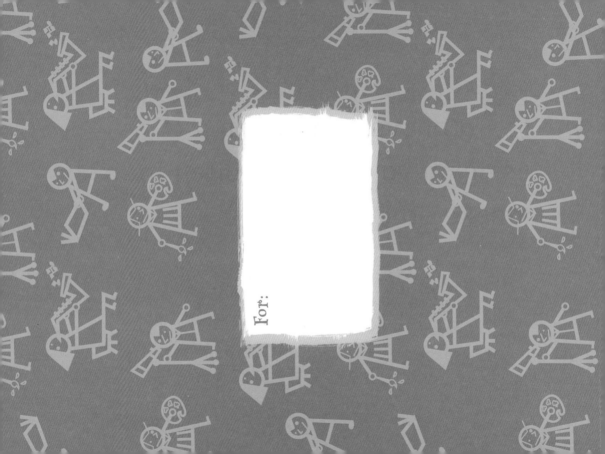

For:

I know more about

_____

because of you. Thanks for
sharing your interests with us.

For:

A little bird told me you are incredible on the _____ field. I'd love to come and see you play sometime.

For:

You read more books than anyone I know! I can't wait to see what you read next.

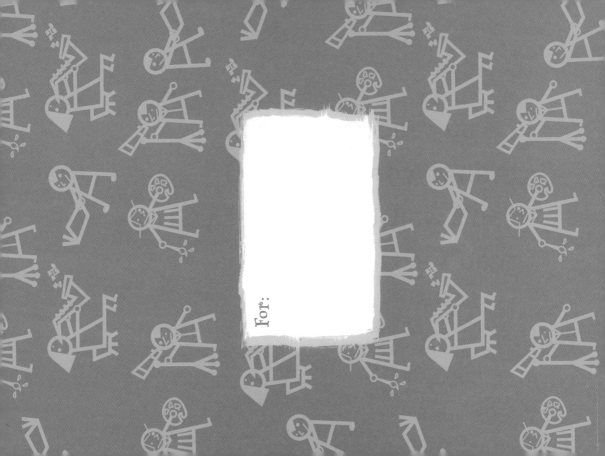

For:

You can always make me laugh! That is a very special talent.

For:

When I see you helping in the classroom it makes me realize what a wonderful person you are becoming. Thank you for all your help.

For:

Thank you for your sweet gift. Gifts from my students are the most precious!

Thank You

For:

Thank you for helping a classmate today. It means so much to know you care.

For:

Thank you for being on your best behavior with the substitute. It makes coming back a real pleasure.

For:

Thank you for being such a good helper during class today. I like being able to count on you.

For:

You made me laugh today! Thank you for making my day brighter.

For:

Thank you for remembering me with a gift. It means so much!

For:

You have such a kind heart. Thank you for sharing it with all of us!

For:

You add so much to our class. Thank you for always doing a great job!

For:

I heard you encourage another student today. Thank you for being such a good friend.

For:

I am so proud of you for respecting others. You set a good example for others to follow.

Show proper respect to everyone.
1 Peter 2:17 NIV

I'm Proud of You

For:

I can tell you're working hard. Keep it up. Remember that I'm here if you need me.

For:

You were kind today when it would have been easier to be mean to someone. You are a great example to others.

Be kind to one another.
Ephesians 4:32 NASB

I'm Proud of You

For:

Y ou did a quality job on your project. You did more than I asked you to do! Excellent work.

For:

You are so creative! I can always tell it's your work even if your name isn't on it.

For:

You were patient today when someone else needed your help. Patience is a gift!

I'm Proud of You

For:

Thank you for being a help to the substitute while I was gone. I knew I could count on you!

For:

You have made great improvement so far this year. I'm so proud of you!

For:

I know _____ is a difficult subject for you. The fact that you are trying so hard means so much. I will help you all I can!

For:

I appreciate that you showed self-control today. I know it's hard not to talk during class.

For:

About the Author

Vicki Caruana is a veteran educator and curriculum designer. She is author of the best-selling books *Apples & Chalkdust* and *Apples & Chalkdust 2*, along with *Prayers from a Teacher's Heart*.

Vicki loves to encourage teachers. She is a featured speaker at conferences for educators in public, private, and homeschool settings. She writes for a wide variety of publications, including *ParentLife*, *Focus on the Family*, *Parenting for High Potential*, and *Becoming Family*. She is a former teacher turned writer who specializes in educational topics for teachers, parents, and children. Vicki seeks to educate and encourage kids and those who live and work with them to strive for excellence.

Vicki is a frequent guest on national radio and television programs. Vicki speaks at educational, parenting, and writers' conferences. She is also often invited to speak at schools and universities. Vicki wants to encourage teachers and teach the rest of American society how to do the same.

Vicki credits her inspiration to her first grade teacher, Mrs. Robinson at Mount Vernon Elementary School, who influenced her decision at age six to become a teacher, and to her family with whom she lives in Colorado Springs, Colorado.

For additional information on seminars, consulting services, to schedule speaking engagements, or to write the author, please address your correspondence to: vcaruana@aol.com or visit her Web site at: www.encourageteachers.com.

Additional copies of this book are available from your local bookstore. Check out other titles from the Apples and Chalkdust series.

Apples and Chalkdust—Inspirations and Encouragement for Teachers
Apples and Chalkdust for Teachers
Apples and Chalkdust #2
Prayers from a Teacher's Heart

If you have enjoyed this book, or it has
impacted your life, we would like to hear from you.
Please contact us at:

Honor Books
An Imprint of Cook Communications Ministries
4050 Lee Vance View
Colorado Springs, Colorado 80918
info@honorbooks.com
www.cookministries.com